The life of Marianne: or, the adventures of the Countess of ***. By M. de Marivaux. Translated from the original French. Volume 1 of 3

Pierre Carlet de Chamblain de Marivaux

PRINT EDITIONS

*The life of Marianne: or, the adventures of the Countess of ***. By M. de Marivaux. Translated from the original French. Volume 1 of 3*

Marivaux, Pierre Carlet de Chamblain de
ESTCID: T105590
Reproduction from British Library
Volumes II and III bear the imprint: "printed for Charles Davis and Paul Vaillant" and are dated respectively 1741 and 1742.
London : printed for Charles Davis, 1736-42.
3v. ; 12°

Eighteenth Century
Collections Online
Print Editions

Gale ECCO Print Editions

Relive history with *Eighteenth Century Collections Online*, now available in print for the independent historian and collector. This series includes the most significant English-language and foreign-language works printed in Great Britain during the eighteenth century, and is organized in seven different subject areas including literature and language; medicine, science, and technology; and religion and philosophy. The collection also includes thousands of important works from the Americas.

The eighteenth century has been called "The Age of Enlightenment." It was a period of rapid advance in print culture and publishing, in world exploration, and in the rapid growth of science and technology – all of which had a profound impact on the political and cultural landscape. At the end of the century the American Revolution, French Revolution and Industrial Revolution, perhaps three of the most significant events in modern history, set in motion developments that eventually dominated world political, economic, and social life.

In a groundbreaking effort, Gale initiated a revolution of its own: digitization of epic proportions to preserve these invaluable works in the largest online archive of its kind. Contributions from major world libraries constitute over 175,000 original printed works. Scanned images of the actual pages, rather than transcriptions, recreate the works *as they first appeared.*

Now for the first time, these high-quality digital scans of original works are available via print-on-demand, making them readily accessible to libraries, students, independent scholars, and readers of all ages.

For our initial release we have created seven robust collections to form one the world's most comprehensive catalogs of 18th century works.

Initial Gale ECCO Print Editions collections include:

History and Geography

Rich in titles on English life and social history, this collection spans the world as it was known to eighteenth-century historians and explorers. Titles include a wealth of travel accounts and diaries, histories of nations from throughout the world, and maps and charts of a world that was still being discovered. Students of the War of American Independence will find fascinating accounts from the British side of conflict.

Social Science

Delve into what it was like to live during the eighteenth century by reading the first-hand accounts of everyday people, including city dwellers and farmers, businessmen and bankers, artisans and merchants, artists and their patrons, politicians and their constituents. Original texts make the American, French, and Industrial revolutions vividly contemporary.

Medicine, Science and Technology

Medical theory and practice of the 1700s developed rapidly, as is evidenced by the extensive collection, which includes descriptions of diseases, their conditions, and treatments. Books on science and technology, agriculture, military technology, natural philosophy, even cookbooks, are all contained here.

Literature and Language

Western literary study flows out of eighteenth-century works by Alexander Pope, Daniel Defoe, Henry Fielding, Frances Burney, Denis Diderot, Johann Gottfried Herder, Johann Wolfgang von Goethe, and others. Experience the birth of the modern novel, or compare the development of language using dictionaries and grammar discourses.

Religion and Philosophy

The Age of Enlightenment profoundly enriched religious and philosophical understanding and continues to influence present-day thinking. Works collected here include masterpieces by David Hume, Immanuel Kant, and Jean-Jacques Rousseau, as well as religious sermons and moral debates on the issues of the day, such as the slave trade. The Age of Reason saw conflict between Protestantism and Catholicism transformed into one between faith and logic -- a debate that continues in the twenty-first century.

Law and Reference

This collection reveals the history of English common law and Empire law in a vastly changing world of British expansion. Dominating the legal field is the *Commentaries of the Law of England* by Sir William Blackstone, which first appeared in 1765. Reference works such as almanacs and catalogues continue to educate us by revealing the day-to-day workings of society.

Fine Arts

The eighteenth-century fascination with Greek and Roman antiquity followed the systematic excavation of the ruins at Pompeii and Herculaneum in southern Italy; and after 1750 a neoclassical style dominated all artistic fields. The titles here trace developments in mostly English-language works on painting, sculpture, architecture, music, theater, and other disciplines. Instructional works on musical instruments, catalogs of art objects, comic operas, and more are also included.

The BiblioLife Network

This project was made possible in part by the BiblioLife Network (BLN), a project aimed at addressing some of the huge challenges facing book preservationists around the world. The BLN includes libraries, library networks, archives, subject matter experts, online communities and library service providers. We believe every book ever published should be available as a high-quality print reproduction; printed on-demand anywhere in the world. This insures the ongoing accessibility of the content and helps generate sustainable revenue for the libraries and organizations that work to preserve these important materials.

The following book is in the "public domain" and represents an authentic reproduction of the text as printed by the original publisher. While we have attempted to accurately maintain the integrity of the original work, there are sometimes problems with the original work or the micro-film from which the books were digitized. This can result in minor errors in reproduction. Possible imperfections include missing and blurred pages, poor pictures, markings and other reproduction issues beyond our control. Because this work is culturally important, we have made it available as part of our commitment to protecting, preserving, and promoting the world's literature.

GUIDE TO FOLD-OUTS MAPS and OVERSIZED IMAGES

The book you are reading was digitized from microfilm captured over the past thirty to forty years. Years after the creation of the original microfilm, the book was converted to digital files and made available in an online database.

In an online database, page images do not need to conform to the size restrictions found in a printed book. When converting these images back into a printed bound book, the page sizes are standardized in ways that maintain the detail of the original. For large images, such as fold-out maps, the original page image is split into two or more pages

Guidelines used to determine how to split the page image follows:

• Some images are split vertically; large images require vertical and horizontal splits.
• For horizontal splits, the content is split left to right.
• For vertical splits, the content is split from top to bottom.
• For both vertical and horizontal splits, the image is processed from top left to bottom right.

THE

LIFE

OF

MARIANNE:

OR,

The ADVENTURES of the Counteſs of ***.

By M. *De MARIVAUX.*

Tranſlated from the Original *French.*

L. O N D O N:

Printed for CHARLES DAVIS in,

Pater-Noſter-Row.

MDCCXXXVI.

ADVERTISEMENT.

AS this History may probably be suspected of having been contrived purposely to amuse the Publick, it may not be improper to acquaint the Reader, that I had it from a Friend who actually found it in the Manner immediately mentioned. Nor had I any other Hand in the Work, than that of having revised and touched a few Places of it, that were too confused and incorrect. The Truth is, that, was this History a meer Fiction, very likely the Form of it would have been different. Marianne's Reflections would be neither so long nor so frequent. It would contain more Facts and less Morality; In short, the Author would have indulged the universal Inclination of the present Age, which, in Books of this Kind, does not relish abundance of Arguments and Reflections. When they read Adventures, it is only for the Sake of the Adventures themselves. But Marianne, when she wrote, did not in the least regard this. She pleased herself in setting down indifferently the whole Compass of her Reflections on every Incident of her

B   Life.

Life. They are long or short, according as the Subject of them pleased her. Very likely the Friend she writes to was as fond of reflecting as herself. Besides, Marianne had forsaken the World, a Kind of Life which gives the Mind a grave and philosophical Turn. In short, this Work is intirely hers, the Alteration of a few Words excepted. We give the Publick the first Part of it at present, and if this be approved, the other being ready shall soon follow.

THE

THE

LIFE

OF

MARIANNE, &c.

BEfore I offer the Publick this Hiftory, I fhall acquaint my Readers, how I came by it.

SIX Months ago I bought a Country Houfe, fome Leagues diftant from *Rennes,* which has for thefe laft thirty Years been in Poffeffion of five or fix different Perfons. As I was making fome Alteration in the firft Apartment, in a Cup-board, that had been contrived in the Corner of a Wall, there was found a Manufcript, of feveral Quires of Paper, containing the following Hiftory, all writ in a Woman's Hand. It was brought to me, and I read it to a couple of Friends, who have continually folicited me to have it printed. I agreed to this, the rather becaufe no Body is characterized in it By the Date, found at the End of the Manufcript, it was writ forty Years ago. We changed the Names

of

of two Perſons mentioned in it, now both dead. Though what is ſaid of them be of no great Conſequence, yet it was thought more adviſeable to conceal their Names.

This ſhort Account is all I had to ſay, and this perhaps is the only Thing of my own, that will ever come to Light, having no Talent for writing.

Let us now take the Hiſtory in Hand. 'Tis a Woman writes her own Life, and her Perſon is unknown. She gives herſelf the Name of *Marianne*, at the Beginning of her Narration. She afterwards ſtiles herſelf a Counteſs, and addreſſes to one of her Friends, whoſe Name is not mentioned.

WHEN I recounted to you a few Particulars of my Life, I did not expect, my dear Friend, that you would require me to give you an Account of the whole, and to make it a Book fit for the Preſs. It muſt be owned, that my Hiſtory is very uncommon: But writing it myſelf will be of no Advantage to the Work, ſince I am defective in Point of Style.

'Tis true the World once thought me witty; But, my Dear, I am of Opinion, that my Sort of Wit is only fit to be uttered, never printed.

We pretty Women, (for I was once of that Number) let us have ever ſo little Wit, it will be thought fuperior to that of the reft of the World. For in that Cafe, Men are no more able to fet a Value on our Words. Gazing, on us while they liften to our Difcourfe, they admire what they hear, for the fake of what they fee.

I knew once an handfome Woman whofe Converfation was reckoned charming and delightful. Her Expreffions were incomparable; her Turns, Nicety and Delicacy itfelf. The beft Judges were tranfported with Pleafure when fhe fpoke. She was fuddenly feized with the Small-Pox, and happened to be extremely pitted, but when fhe appeared again, what is wonderful! All her Wit was become a downright troublefome Chit-chat. Whence you may judge how much her Senfe was before indebted to her pretty Face. And 'tis not unlikely, that on the fame Account, I got the Reputation of a Wit. I remember well how my Eyes looked at that Time, and I think truly the Wit was theirs not mine.

How many Times did I catch myfelf faying Things, which of themfelves would never have ftood Trial! Had it not been for a little coquetifh, wanton Air, that accompanied them, I fhould never have been praifed fo much as I was; and to tell you the Truth, I really believe, that, had all my Conceits been reduced to their intrinfic Value by the Small-Pox,

they

they would have fuffered very great Abate-ments.

For inftance, but a Month ago, you put me in Mind of my being one Day at a Feaft, (tho' 'tis twelve Years fince) when the Company were fo prodigioufly diverted with my Sprightlinefs; believe me, my Dear, I was indeed a perfect giddy Thing. Nay, I frequently played the Fool, for no other Purpofe, but to fee how far Men might be our Dupes. None of my Snares were too coarfe to catch them, and you may be fure that the very fame Extravagancies uttered by an homely Woman, would have made her pafs for one that came out of *Bedlam*. And who knows but the Agreeablenefs of my Perfon was neceffary to make the beft Things I could fay tolerable? For now that all my Charms are vanifhed, I perceive my Parts are looked upon as ordinary and common enough, though I am far better pleafed with myfelf than I ever was. However, fince you will have me write my own Hiftory, as a Token of my Friendfhip towards you, I will indulge your Defires; For I had rather venture tiring you, than refufe you any Thing.

I juft now mentioned a Stile, but if you afk me what that is, really the Queftion will remain unanfwered. Pray, what muft an Author do to fall upon a Stile? Is that of Books the beft? What then makes me
diflike

diſlike it ſo much in moſt of them? Do
you think that of my Letters tolerable?
Why then, I will write this juſt as I would
do a Letter.   But be ſure to keep your
Promiſe, and never let any Mortal know
who I am, for I am reſolved to be unknown to all the World but you.

When I was but fifteen Years younger
than I am now, I never had been informed whether I was of a mean or a noble Extraction, a Baſtard or Legitimate. I own
this looks like the Beginning of a Romance.   Neverthelefs, what I tell you has
nothing in it romantick, and is juſt as I
had it from thoſe that brought me up.

A Stage-coach going to *Bourdeaux*, was
attacked on the Road by Robbers.   Two
Gentlemen that were in it offered Reſi-
ſtance, and had actually wounded one of theſe
Villains, but they were killed by them at
laſt, with three Perſons more. Our Coachman and Poſtillion underwent the ſame
Fate, and there was none left in the Coach
but a Prebendary of *Sens* and I, not ap-
pearing to be above two or three Years
of Age.   The Prebendary fled, while
I, who had tumbled into the Boot, was
roaring moſt fearfully.   For I was half
ſmothered by a Woman who being wounded and attempting to eſcape fell backward
into the Boot, expired on me, and almoſt
cruſhed me to Death.

The Horfes ftood ftock ftill, and I re-mained in that difmal Condition for a whole Quarter of an Hour, continually fhriek-ing, without being able to get rid of my Load.

You muft know, that there were among the Dead two Women, one of whom was handfome and about twenty Years of Age, and the other feemed to be forty. The former was dreffed like a Gentlewoman, and the latter like a Chamber-maid.

If one of them was my Mother, very likely it was the younger and the better dreffed, for thofe that faw her lying dead by me, fancied that I favoured her a little; befides my Clothes were too rich for the Daughter of a Chamber-maid.

I forgot to tell you that one of our Gen-tlemen's Footmen efcaped crofs the Fields wounded, and dropped down quite fpent at the Entrance of a neighbouring Village, where he died without declaring to whom he belonged. All they could get out of him before he expired was, that his Mafter and Miftrefs had been juft murder-ed; But this was no Information as to the Cafe in queftion.

Whilft I was lamenting under the Body of the younger Woman, who was dead, five or fix Officers came by riding Poft, who feeing a few People dead by the Coach which ftood there ftill, and hearing

the

the Cries of a Child within, were furprifed at the difmal Sight, and moved either by that Curiofity, which horrid Scenes are apt to raife in us, or in order to fee what Child was crying, and whether they could any way affift it, came up to the Coach, and having looked in, faw another Man killed, and the Woman dead in the Boot, where by my Cries they foon judged I was.

One of them, as they fince have owned, was abfolutely for withdrawing; But another moved with Compaffion for me, prevented it, and alighting came firft to the Coach, and opened the Boot wherein I was. The others followed him, but were fhocked by a new Scene of Horror. For this dead Lady lay with one fide of her Face upon mine, and had bathed me with her Blood. They removed her and took me all over Blood, from under that unfortunate Woman.

The next Queftion was, what they fhould do with me, and whither I fhould be carried. They faw a fmall Town at a Diftance, and refolving to carry me thither, they gave me to a Servant of theirs, who wrapt me in a Cloak.

Their Intention was to deliver me to the Vicar of the Place, to fee out for fome Body charitable enough to take Care of me. But the Vicar, to whom the whole Village was ready to conduct them, was

gone

gone to vifit another Clergyman.   There was no Body in his Houfe but his Sifter, a very pious Woman, whofe Compaffion for me was fo great, that fhe took me in, till fhe could prevail with her Brother to keep me.   There was moreover an Account taken of all thefe Particulars, and drawn up by a Notary that lived in the Place.

Every one of my Conductors generoufly gave me fome Money, which was put into a Purfe, and delivered into the Hands of the Vicar's Sifter, and then they all departed.

Every one of thefe Particulars I had from the Vicar's Sifter.

I don't doubt but they fill you with Horror.   No one, I think, can begin Life more unfortunately, or under ftranger Difafters.   By good Luck, I was not myfelf when I underwent them: For a Child that's but two Years old can hardly be faid to be itfelf.

What became of the Coach or of the poor murdered Travellers I will not mention being nothing to my Purpofe.   Some of the Murderers were apprehended three or four Days after, but what added to my Misfortune was, that nothing was found about thofe they had killed that might reveal the Secret of my Birth   In vain the Regifter of the Names of thofe that travel in Stage-
Coaches

Coaches was fearched.   They found indeed who they all were, except one Gentleman and a Lady, whofe Name founding
like that of Foreigners could be no Information, and who knows but that they had
concealed their real Name.   All one could
learn from the Regifter was, that they had
taken five Places in the Coach, two for
themfelves, one for a little Girl, and two
more for a Footman and a Chamber-maid,
who were likewife affaffinated.

By all this, the Secret of my Birth could
no way be found out, and the Charity of
Mankind became the only Relation I had.

The Greatnefs of my Misfortune procured me confiderable Helps in the Houfe
of the Vicar, who agreed with his Sifter
to keep me.

People came to fee me from all the
neighbouring Places.   Every Body wanted to be acquainted with my Phyfiognomy,
which had excited an univerfal Curiofity.
They imagined, that there was fomething
in my Face relating to my Adventure. All
took a Kind of a romantick Fancy to me.
Befides I was very pretty, and my Air
quite engaging.   You can't imagine, how
much all thefe Things were to my Advantage, and what a Turn of Elegance and Delicacy it gave to the tender Concern every
one had for me.   An unfortunate little
Princefs never could have been careffed

more nobly. Nay, the Compaſſion I raiſed in every Mind ſeemed rather Reverence than Pity.

But nothing was comparable to the Concern the Ladies expreſſed for me; for they were always making me Preſents of the fineſt and genteeleſt Dreſſes, in which they ſtrove to outvye one another.

Since which Time the Vicar, who was of a very good Family, and a Man of Wit, though a Country Clergy-man, uſed to ſay very often, that he never heard thoſe Ladies uſe the Word *Charity*, in all they then did for me, becauſe the Expreſſion was too hard, and might have ſhocked the Nicety of their Sentiments for me.

Whenever they ſpoke of me, they never called me *that little Girl*; it was always *that lovely Child*.

When they mentioned my Parents, no doubt they were Foreigners and of prodigious great Quality in their own Country. The Thing could not be otherwiſe, and they were as ſure of it, as if they had been Eye-witneſſes of every Circumſtance they were pleaſed to imagine. There was a little Story given out about me, which had been amplified by the Extravagancies of every one that told it, and of which they were afterwards as fully convinced, as if they had not been the Authors of it themſelves.

But

But all things come to an End in this World, and the fineſt Sentiments have their Period as well as other Things. As my Adventure grew ſtale, it ceaſed to ſtrike their Fancy. An Habit of ſeeing me, diſſipated the Imaginations which had been ſo beneficial to me. It exhauſted the Satisfaction they took in loving me. As it had been but a tranſitory Pleaſure, their lovely Child in ſix Months time was dwindled into a poor fatherleſs and motherleſs Creature, and one with whom they no longer ſcrupled to uſe the Word *Charity*, for they ſaid I had a Title to their moſt charitable Diſpoſitions: All the Vicars in the Neighbourhood recommended me to their Pariſhioners; for the Gentleman with whom I lived had no Eſtate. But the Religion of the Ladies was of much leſs Service to me than their Extravagance had been: For I made little or no Advantage of it, and had not the Vicar and his Siſter taken the tendereſt Inclination for me, my Condition would have been very deplorable.

That Gentlewoman brought me up as ſhe would have done her own Child. I told you already, that her Brother and ſhe were of a very good Family. A Report went, that a Law-ſuit had exhauſted all their Fortune, and that he had ſince retired to this Living, whither his Siſter followed him,

him, as they were very fond of one another.

A Country Vicar's Niece or Sifter is
moft commonly an unbred aukward Coun-
try-like Woman.

But this was a Perfon very different,
for good Senfe, Politenefs and Virtue
were united in her in the higheft Degree.

I remember that many Times when fhe
looked on me, fhe could not reftrain her
Tears, at the Thoughts of my Difafter:
But then in Return I loved her as I would
have done my own Mother. I muft own
too, that all my Ways were graceful and
engaging, much above thofe of the common Run of Children. I was of a mild
and gay Temper, with a fine Gefture and
Face, which gave great Hopes of an agreeable Phyfiogmony, and indeed it anfwered
thofe Hopes perfectly well.

I pafs over in Silence the whole Time of
my Education and Infancy, during which
I learned to do a thoufand little Works,
which have fince proved a very great Help
to me.

I was much about fifteen, (for my Age
might eafily be miftaken) when one of the
Vicar's Coufins, who had no other Heir
except his Sifter and him, writ from *Paris*
that he was dangeroufly ill. He had already given them frequent Information of
his ill State of Health: But he preffc

them

them in this Letter to come to *Paris* in all
haste, if they had a Mind to see him before
his Death. As the Vicar was very exact
in performing the Duties of his Function,
he determined not to leave his Cure, and
sent his Sister to *Paris.*

At first, she scrupled taking me with
her; but two Days before she went, as she
saw me very much dejected, and heard
me sigh most sadly, *Marianne,* said she,
take Courage, since you so much dread
my Absence, I will not be against your
going along with me, and I hope my Brother will consent. I have even a Prospect
for you. My Intention is to put you
a Prentice to some Tradeswoman, for
it is time for you to think of doing
something. As long as we live my Brother
and I will always help you, not to mention what we may leave you when we
die. But that will never be sufficient to
maintain you; For we can leave you very
little. I don't believe our Cousin to whom
I am going is very rich, and we must think
of chusing for you such a Station as will
be a Settlement. All this I tell you, my
dear *Marianne,* because you begin to have
Judgment, and I would fain have the
Comfort, before I die, of seeing you mar-
ried to some honest Man, or at least in the
Way of being so, to your Advantage. It is
but just indeed, that I should have that
Satisfaction.   I ran

I ran into her Arms upon this. I wept heartily, and so did she, for she was throughly good natur'd, and I was my self of a sweet Disposition; nor am I yet much altered.

Hereupon the Vicar came in. What is the Matter, said he, Sister, I believe *Marianne* is crying? She up and told him the Subject of our Conversation, and the Design she had to carry me to *Paris.* With all my Heart, said he; But if she stays there, I doubt we shall see her no more. The Thought of that makes my Heart ake; For I love the poor Child dearly: We brought her up: I am grown very old, and this may be my last farewell.

Nothing, as you see, was more moving than this Conversation. I could make no other Reply than Sighs, Sobs and Groans, which moved them still more, upon which the good old Man came up to me; *Marianne,* said he, you shall go with my Sister, since it is for your Advantage, which I must prefer to any other Consideration. We have been to you in lieu of your Parents, whom it pleased God you never knew, nor any of your Family. Therefore, never venture to do any thing while we are alive, without our Advice, and if my Sister can leave you at *Paris* in a good Place (otherwise you shall come back with her) do you write to us, whenever

you

you ftand in need of our Counfels. As for our Love and Affiftance, 'tis what you fhall never want.

I fhall not repeat you all he faid to me before we went; for all thofe little infignificant Particulars of my Youth have no Doubt tired you, as they are of little or no Concern, and I long to come to more material Things. I have a great many to tell you, and I cannot but have the greateft Love and Efteem for you, fince I have taken upon me to give you a Narration, which will not be very fhort. I fhall furely wafte a great deal of Paper in Scribling ; But I will not think of it, for fear my Lazinefs fhould take the Alarm. Let us then go on freely, and never mind it.

We then fet forward, the Vicar's Sifter and I, and arrived at *Paris*. We were obliged to crofs the greateft Part of the Town, before we could reach the Houfe of their abovementioned Relation.

My Amazement at the Sight of that large, populous and noify Town far exceeds all Defcription. It was the Empire of the Moon to me. I was perfectly out of my Wits. I had loft my Memory. All I could do was juft to move my Body, and open my Eyes. I was, in fhort, a meer gaping Machine.

However, I came to my felf again before I was fet down, and began to enjoy
the

the Objects of my Amazement. My Sentiments were no longer a Paradox; and I began to be overjoy'd to fee my felf where I was. The Air I then breathed revived my Spirits; for there feemed to be an agreeable Sympathy betwixt my Fancy and the Objects that offered. I guefled that this vaft Croud of Varieties contained an inexhauftible Source of Pleafures yet unknown to me. I thought in fhort all manner of Delight centered there. Pray, was not this a true womanifh Fancy, and even an Omen of all my future Adventures?

They were foon foretold me by *Deftiny.* (For, muft not *Deftiny* have always a Share in a Woman's Hiftory?) We found the Coufin we were going to had been dead, not above four and twenty Hours.

But this was not all; for every Apartment in his Houfe was fealed up. He had held feveral Offices under the State, and 'twas faid his Debts far exceeded his Fortune.

How they made that out, I won't pretend to fay, it being an Affair much beyond my Capacity. All I know of it is, that we could not be admitted into his Houfe, where all was feized, and that after many Debates in the Compafs of three full Months, they convinced us at laft that there was not one Penny of what

he

he had left for us, and that it was a thou-
sand Pities he had left no more, for the
better Discharge of his Debts.

Had we not then made a very fine Journey of it? The Vicar's Sister was so much
vexed at it, that she fell sick at our Lodg-
ings.

All her Grief, alas! was for my sake
alone. She hoped that this Incident would
make her able to do me good. Besides,
this fruitless Journey had almost exhausted
her Purse. The Money she had brought
with her was considerably diminished; it
decreased every Day, and her Brother, who
had nothing but his Living to depend on,
could not send her any more, without
great Difficulty. But her Sickness was our
great Grievance. Lord! what a moving
Sight she was!

She did nothing but sigh every Minute.
The dear Woman never loved me so much
as she then did, because she had never
seen me in so deplorable a Condition. On
my Part, I comforted and caressed her continually, and indeed without the least Af-
fectation; for all my Sentiments were honest and full of Gratitude. My Heart was
forwarder and more delicate than my Wit,
though this was pretty ripe too.

You may judge she had informed the
Vicar of all our Misfortunes: But there
are fatal Periods, wherein all Sorts of Dis-
asters

afters rufh in upon us (and this we are forced to think from Experience.) The honeft old Gentleman, as he went to vifit one of his Fellow-Clergymen, had the Misfortune to get a Fall, fix Weeks after we went; A very dangerous Accident for an old Man. He had not been able to ftir out of his Bed ever fince, but lingered there, when the fatal News came from his Sifter. He was feized with fo many Infirmities at once, that he was in a Manner obliged to refign his Living, and name his own Succeffor. They affected his Mind as well as his Body. He had Time however to fend us a little more Money, after which he was to be looked upon as good as dead.

The Thought of all this fills me ftill with Horror. The Earth is fure a Country very foreign to virtuous Minds, fince they are perpetually tortured upon it.

We had almoft loft all Hopes of his Sifter's Recovery, when we received this fatal News. She gave a loud Shriek at reading of the Letter and fainted.

For my Part I melted in Tears. I called for Help; fhe came again to her felf; but did not fhed a fingle Tear. From that Moment I obferved in her nothing but a couragious Refignation to the Decrees of Providence. Her Heart was all Courage. The uneafy Fondnefs fhe had
before

before for me, became on a fudden a virtuous Affection, and fhe refigned me with
all imaginable Confidence into the Hands
of him, who is the Mafter of all Events.

When fhe came to her felf, and we were
alone, fhe bid me come to her. Pray,
my dear Friend, give me leave to relate
here a Part of her Difcourfe, the Re-
membrance of which will always be dear
to me, for thefe are the laft Words I
heard from her.

" *Marianne*, faid fhe, I have no more a
" Brother; for though mine be not yet
" dead, with regard to you and I he is
" as good. I perceive that you will alfo
" lofe me foon. But though your Con-
" dition be extremely deplorable, it is
" fome Comfort to think, that it is God's
" Will. He aims at things much more
" to your Advantage than any I could
" ever intend. Perhaps I fhall lye a while
" in this lingering Condition: Not that
" it is improbable, but that the very firft
" Time I faint 'twill carry me off. (This
" alas! was but too true) I dare not, conti-
" nued fhe, truft you with the Reft of my
" Money; for you are too young, and
" liable to be deceiv'd. I will deliver it
" into the Hands of the Monk who vifits
" me every Day. You fhall go fetch
" him to Morrow, that I may fpeak
" to him. After this laft Care taken of
" you,

" you, the only Thing I have to recom-
" mend to you is to be inflexibly virtuous
" and honeft. I have brought you up
" in the Love of Virtue. Do you but
" conftantly reflect on your Education,
" and be affured, my dear *Marianne*,
" that you will by fo doing become pof-
" feffed of the greateft Treafure that could
" poffibly be left to you : For it will
" be a Treafure to your very Soul. 'Tis
" true, it won't prevent your being poor
" as to Fortune, and you may live per-
" haps in very great Straits. Not that it
" is unlikely, but that God will reward
" your Virtue and Honefty even in this
" World. Virtuous Minds are fcarce,
" but the Lovers of Virtue are in great
" Plenty. And they are the more fo, be-
" caufe there is no doing without them
" even in this World. For inftance, no
" Man is willing to marry any but an ho-
" neft Woman. Let her Condition be ne-
" ver fo mean, 'tis no matter, there is no
" Difhonour attends it : But if fhe be rich
" and wants Virtue, Shame will be the
" Portion fhe brings to her Hufband. Be-
" lieve me, Child, Men will always be of
" this Mind, for it is not in their Nature
" to be otherwife. Therefore, be but
" virtuous, and never doubt but that you
" will one Day or other find a Hufband.
" Befides, is not Virtue the fweeteft and

" moft

" moſt comfortable Companion, to ſuch
" as cheriſh it in their Hearts, even to
" ſuch as live in a conſtant Scene of Mi-
" ſery? So ſoon is their Poverty at an
" end! ſo ſhort is Life! The great Scor-
" ners of what we call Honeſty, neverthe-
" leſs make ſo very free with ſuch Women
" as ſuffer themſelves to be ſeduced;
" They take Advantage of their Weakneſs
" with ſo ſteady an Impudence; They
" puniſh them ſo very ſeverely for the
" Diſorders they have brought upon them;
" They are ſo ſenſible of their being deſ-
" titute of all Defence, and find them ſo
" intirely degraded and deſpicable, by the
" Loſs of that Virtue which they ſet ſo
" light by and ridiculed, that it is only
" for want of reflecting, that any Woman
" grows lewd. For who would think on it
" a Moment, and chuſe to get rid of Po-
" verty, at the ſevere Rate of being infa-
" mous and deſpiſed——.

One of the Houſe came in upon this
nd ſtopped her. Perhaps you will aſk
what my Anſwer to it was? Indeed nothing;
for I was not able to utter a Word. Her
Diſcourſe, and the Thoughts of her approaching Death had quite turned my
Brains. I held her Arm, and kiſſed it a
houſand Times, but could do nothing elſe.

However, I loſt not a Syllable of what
he ſaid, and it made ſuch an Impreſſion

on my Mind, that I believe I have here
repeated every individual Word of it to
you. I was then fifteen Years and a half
at leaft, and was apprehenfive enough,
not to want any Explanation of all this.

Let us now come to the Ufe I made of
it. Lord, how many Extravagancies am
I entering upon! How deplorable is the
Condition of Men, who never begin to act
wifely, but when it can hardly be thought
a Virtue in them. When they fay, fuch
an one is at Years of Difcretion; pray,
what do they mean by it? Sure the Expreffion is very faulty ; For the Years of
Difcretion meant, are more properly Years
of Madnefs. When Reafon once comes
on, it is a moft beautiful Jewel, often
looked at, much valued, but never made
ufe of. Pray, my dear, bear with thefe
tranfient Reflections. I fhall always make
fome of them by the by. The Privilege
of reflecting is of right but too much mine,
fince it is the Price of fo many Extravagancies. Now let us proceed. Till now
I had been at the Expence of others, but
fhall foon be at my own.

The Vicar's Sifter had told me, fhe
fufpected fhe fhould go off with her next
Fainting: And alas! it prov'd a Prophecy.

I would not go to Bed that Night. I
fat up with her. She flept pretty well till
two in the Morning, but after that I heard
her

her groan, and running to her Bed, I spoke to her, but she was already speech-less. She only squeezed my Hand, and looked like one expiring.

I was then suddenly seized with a Fright, proceeding from the Certainty of losing her. I presently lost my Senses. Lord, how terrible was then the State of my Mind! Methought, that the whole World was a Desart, in which I was ready to be left alone. I then perceived how dearly I loved her, and how tender she had been towards me. All these Things were in an instant presented to my Imagination, and struck me so to the Heart, that I was raving with the Thought of them.

Good God! how much Grief are we liable to ! What Trouble and Sense of Mi-sery fall upon our Minds ! I must confess, that my having thus endured the highest Degree of Grief possible, has always shocked me violently, whenever I thought of it. To that Thought I even owe the vast Relish I have now for Retirement.

I am not capable of arguing in the Philosophic Strain, nor do I much care, for I believe it is little more than Words in the main. Those I have heard argue in that manner are, no doubt, very witty ; but I be-lieve nevertheless, that on certain Topicks, they resemble those News-mongers, which

broach

broach Falfities, for want of real Occurren-
ces, or alter the Advices they receive, when
they like them not. For my part, I think
that Experience is the only Thing, can give
us any good Account of our felves, and
that we ought not to depend too rafhly on
thofe our Wit is pleafed to contrive, for I
take that to be capricious enough.

But to return, I am quite afhamed of
what I have been faying, though I was
fond enough of it, fo long as it lafted.
'Tis likely I fhall in time come to relifh
the holding of an Argument. For in every thing the firft Steps, they fay, are only
difficult. And pray, why fhould I not
argue? Is it becaufe I am but an illiterate
Woman? Good Senfe fure is of no Sex. I
don't pretend to give others any Inftructi-
ons, for I am already turned of fifty ; and a
very honeft learned Gentleman told me the
other Day, that though I knew nothing,
yet I was not more ignorant than thofe
who were much better Scholars. I fay this
after a Virtuofo of the firft Rank. For
thefe Gentlemen, as elated as they are with
their Learning, have fometimes Fits of
Sincerity, wherein they cannot help fpeaking Truth, and are fo diffatisfied with
their ufual Prefumption, that they quit it,
in order to draw a little frefh Air, under
the Shelter of a convenient Ignorance. It
eafes

eafes them of their Burden, juft as I have eafed my felf of mine, in thus declaring my Opinion of them.

I was feized with the moft weighty Grief, when I faw this virtuous Woman, to whom I was fo much indebted, was expiring. For though fhe had a thoufand Times told me of her approaching Death, I never imagined, that her Sicknefs would fo determine.

The whole Houfe rang again with my Shrieks and Lamentations. They alarmed all the Family. The Landlord and his Wife fufpecting what the Matter was, got up and knock'd at the Room Door. I opened it without knowing what I did. They fpake to me; but my Cries were the only Anfwer I made them. They foon apprehended the Caufe of my Grief. They tried to affift the poor expiring Creature: And who knows but fhe was already gone, for fhe was motionlefs. But half an Hour after, they were pofitive fhe was dead. The Servants came up with Hurry and Clamour, during which I loft my Senfes in a Swoon. I was carried into the next Room without perceiving it. What a Condition I was afterwards in, I will not inform you. You may eafily guefs, and the Recital fills me ftill with Sorrow and Melancholy.

Now

Now was I left alone with no other Guide but the Experience of a Girl of fifteen or thereabout. As the poor dead Woman had owned me for her Niece, and as I feemed to have Underftanding, they gave me a verbal Account of all they faid was found about her, which would not have required a more formal Proceeding, had they even given me up the whole. But a part of the Linnen was ftollen, with fome other Trifles, and I believe they took the Value of two hundred, out of near four hundred Livres the deceafed had left. I complained of it, but in fuch mild Terms, that it availed no more than my Silence would have done. My Afflic-tion was fo very exceffive, that I cared for nothing in the World. As I had no Friend left, to concern himfelf either for me or my Life, I had no Regard to it my felf. And this Turn of Mind put me into fuch a State as made it look like Tranquillity, but alas! how lamentable is fuch feeming Calmnefs! Indeed the greateft Tranfports of Rage and Defpair are lefs to be pitied.

Every one in the Family feemed con-cerned for me, and did all they could to comfort me under a Difafter, of which they had made their Advantage. A kind of People the World fwarms with. For generally, none exprefs a greater Defire of

alle vi

alleviating our Troubles, than thofe who caufe or get any thing by them.

I let them difpofe of feveral things for which they gave me what they thought fit, and there were already fourteen Days, fince my dear Aunt, as they called her, (and I would fain term her my dear Mother, or rather my only Friend, there being no Title but muft yield to that, nor any Heart fo tender or fo unfhaken as one infpired by true and folid Friendfhip.) I fay, there were already fourteen Days, fince my deareft Friend was dead, and I had been all the while in this Lodging, without knowing or caring what fhould become of me; when the Monk already mentioned, who often ufed to vifit the de-ceafed, and had himfelf been very fick, came again to afk how fhe did. He was very forry to hear of her being dead; and as he was the only Man that knew the Secret of my Birth, which the Deceafed had thought proper to reveal to him, and as I was fenfible that he knew it, I faw him with great Satisfaction.

My Misfortune, and the great Uncon-cernednefs I fhewed for my felf in thefe aftonifhing Circumftances extremely mov-ed him. He fpoke to me of it in the moft affecting manner, and reprefented to me the dangerous Confequences of my ftay-ing any longer in this Houfe alone, and

without

without one Soul that would own me.
And indeed I was very much expofed by
my Situation; for my Perfon was perfectly
agreeable, and I was of an Age in which
Beauty is the more engaging, becaufe in
full Bloom, and entirely free from Af-
fectation.

His Difcourfe took Effect. It made me
fenfible of the Danger of my Condition,
and I began to be apprehenfive of what
fhould become of me. This Thought
raifed a thoufand uneafy Fancies in my
Mind. Pray, faid I to him all in Tears,
Whither fhall I go? No Soul on Earth
knows me. I am neither the Daughter
nor Relation of any Man living. To
whom fhall I apply for Help, or who is
obliged to affift me? What fhall I do
when I leave this Houfe? The Money I
have won't laft me long. Befides, it may
be taken from me, and this is the firft
time I ever had any of my own to fpend.

The good old Monk was at a lofs how
to make me a Reply. Methought that
I even began to be a very great Burden to
him by intreating him to direct me. And
thefe are a fort of People, who after they
have once fpoke to you, or given you
their Advice, have done all they are able
to do.

Going into the Country again, would
have been an extravagant Thing. For it
was

was no longer a Refuge for me, and I could find no other Friend there, but an old infirm crazy Man, who had fold all he had left to fend us the laft Money we had received from him, and who had nothing elfe to do but to end his Days in Dependance on a Succeffor, who was as great a Stranger to me as I was to him, or at leaft cared little for me. There was then no Protection to be hoped for on that fide ; a Thought that frightned me almoft to Diftraction.

The Monk, after having rack'd his own Imagination, thought at laft of a noble, charitable and pious Gentleman, who, he faid, had entirely devoted himfelf to virtuous Actions, and to whom he promifed to recommend me the very next Day. But the *next Day* would not do with one who had loft all her Wits, and was quite mad with the Thought of ftaying for Relief any longer. I cried moft defperately. He offered to go more than once ; but I always held him, and threw my felf at his Feet. No *next Day*, faid I. If you don't get me out of this Houfe now, you will prefently throw me into the utmoft Defpair. For God's fake don't go. What would you have me to do in a Place, where they have already taken part of my Money from me ? And ten to one but they will take the reft this Night. I may be run

away

away with. I am in Fear of my Life. I dread every Thing. Be affured I fhall die, rather than ftay a Moment longer here. If you go without me, I fhall certainly flee at all Adventures. And would not this be Matter of Grief to you?

The Monk, who never was more at a Lofs, feeing he could by no Means get rid of me, fell into a profound Study; and then taking a Pen and Ink, wrote a Word to the Gentleman he had told me of. The Letter he read to me was extremely preffing; for he intreated him on his Religion to haften to us with all Speed. God, faid he, has here prepared for you the moft charitable, moft meritorious and moft acceptable Action in his Sight, of any you ever did in your Life. But to perfuade him the more he mentioned my Age, Sex and Beauty, with the fatal Confequences they might poffibly have, either from my own Weaknefs, or the Wickednefs of others.

When the Letter was writ, I fent it as it was directed: And while we waited for an Anfwer, I kept him in View, being fully refolved not to lye that Night in the Houfe. Nor could I tell what it was I apprehended, which was the very Reafon of my Fears being fo very great. All I know is, that I fancied the Face of my Landlord, which I had not taken much Notice of before, was none of the beft. His

His Wife, methought, had a furly
gloomy Look, and the Servants feemed to
me fo many ill natured Rogues; in fhort,
all together made me tremble. Nor could
I longer live in fuch a horrid State of
Mind; for then my Imagination reprefented to me moft dreadful Scenes. I had
nothing in View but Swords, Daggers,
Affaffinations, Robberies, Infults, and o-
ther the like Pieces of Villany. Lord!
how cold my Blood ran at the Thoughts
of the Dangers I fancied my felf in! For
whenever an ill Imagination is upon the
Wing, deplorable is the Mind haraffed
by it.

I was entertaining the Monk with my
melancholy Fancies, when the Man whom
we had fent on our Errand returned, and
told us, that the Coach of the abovementioned virtuous Gentleman was waiting for
us below, and that it was impoffible for
him, either to write or come himfelf, becaufe he was taken up with earneft Bufinefs,
when he received the Letter. I packed off
in an Inftant, like one who had efcaped
the greateft Danger of her Life. I bad.
my horrid Landlord and Landlady come
up: And in reality their Look was none of
the moft engaging, and Imagination had
but little to do, to find them perfectly dif-
agreeable. One thing is very certain, *viz.*
That I have remembred their Faces ever

C 5   fince·

ſince. Methinks I ſee them ſtill, and could draw their Pictures; and I have known ſeveral honeſt People, whom I could not abide, becauſe their Phyſiognomies happened in ſome Reſpect to reſemble theirs.

I then went into the Coach with the Monk, and we were ſoon at the abovementioned Gentleman's. He was a Man between fifty and ſixty, yet ſufficiently genteel, very rich, and of a mild but grave Countenance, mixt with an Air of Mortification, which was predominant over a good Complexion, and happy Plight of Body.

He gave us a kind and free Reception, and no other Compliment than that of embracing the Monk. He once caſt his Eyes upon me, and then deſired us to ſit down.

My Heart fluttered all the while, and I was quite out of Countenance. I durſt not look up, for the Girl's Self-love was ſtupified and quite diſconcerted. Well, ſaid our Gentleman, who wanted to begin the Converſation, and had taken the Monk by the Hand, ſqueezing it with a devout Compunction, what's the Matter? In Anſwer to this, the Monk gave him my Hiſtory. Lord, replied he, what an odd Adventure! and how deplorable is this young Woman's Situation! Sure, you was much in the right, continued he, addreſſing himſelf to the Monk, when you writ me

me

me Word, that doing her Service, was the
beſt Action that ever could be done. I am
indeed of the ſame Opinion, for a thouſand good Reaſons. She ſtands in greater
Need of Help than any other of her Sex.
And I thank you heartily, for having
pitched on me for that Purpoſe. I bleſs
the Moment in which God inſpired you
to apply to me on ſuch an Occaſion: For
I am intirely affected with what I have
heard. Come, let us conſider a little how
we ſhall go about it. My dear Child!
ſaid he, in a cordial and charitable manner, what Age are you? At this Queſtion
I began to ſigh, without being able to utter one Word. Don't ſuffer your ſelf to
be thus caſt down with Grief, ſaid he;
Take Courage, for I deſire nothing more
than to ſerve you. Beſides, God is our
Sovereign Lord, whom we are to praiſe
for every Thing he does. Tell-me then
what Age you think you may be of. Fifteen and a half, ſaid I, and perhaps a little
more. Really, ſaid he, one wou'd be apt
to think her older; but her Looks make
me have a good Opinion of her Sentiments and Wit. They even ſhew her to
be of a noble Extraction. Indeed her
Misfortune is very great. How impene-
trable are the Deſigns of Providence
to us!

But, let us now mind the main Affair,

added

he, after he had thus inwardly adored the
Decrees of Heaven.   As you have no Fortune, we muſt know what ſort of Imployment you would chuſe for your ſelf.
Pray, had your deceaſed Friend taken no
Reſolutions on that Head? Her Intention,
ſaid I, was to put me Apprentice to ſome
Trade.   Very well, replied he, I approve
of her Deſign ; but do you likewiſe approve of it your ſelf? Speak freely ; for
there are ſeveral things that may perhaps
fit you.   For inſtance, I have a Siſter,
who is a very reaſonable Woman, and alſo
rich. She has juſt loſt a Gentlewoman, who
had been with her a great while, and to
whom ſhe would certainly have done much
good, for ſhe loved her tenderly.   If you
would ſucceed her, I am ſure my Siſter
would receive you with Pleaſure.

This Propoſal made me bluſh. Alas ! Sir,
ſaid I, though I am deſtitute of every
Thing, and quite ignorant of my Extraction, methinks, I would chuſe to die, rather than live with any as a Servant ; and
if my Parents were alive, very likely I
ſhould have Servants of my own, inſtead
of being a Servant my ſelf.

I made him this Reply with a very melancholy Air, and then ſhedding a few Tears,
Since I am forced, ſaid I, ſighing and ſobbing bitterly, to work for my Bread, I
ſhall always prefer the meaneſt of Trades

to that Condition, even though I were fure
to make my Fortune by it. Ah! my dear
Child, faid he, pray be eafy. I approve
of your way of thinking. It is a Sign your
Sentiments are not mean. That fort of
Pride no doubt is not to be blamed: But
it muft not be carried to Excefs, for then
it would be no longer reafonable. Let
the Conjectures of your being born of noble Parents be never fo probable, yet do
they fall fhort of Certainty*; and this is
what you are to build upon. However,
we fhall act according to the Views of your
departed Friend. 'Tis true, it will coft
more, becaufe your Board muft be paid
for every Year; but 'tis no matter; you
fhall be provided for this very Day. I will
take you now to my Linnen draper, to
whom I am fure you will be very wel-
come. Now are you fatisfied? Yes, Sir,
faid I, and you may depend on it, that I
fhall never forget your Kindnefs towards
me. Be fure to make your Advantage of
it, faid the Monk, who had been filent
during the whole Dialogue, and let your
Conduct be fuch as will recompence this
Gentleman, for the Care his Piety induces
him to take of you. I am much afraid,
replied he with a devout and feeming fcrupulous Affection, that it will be no Merit
in me to help her, for my being too much
moved at her Misfortunes.

He

He then got up, and said; Don't let us lose Time, Madam: It grows late: Let us make haste to the Gentlewoman I have mentioned. Now, Father, said he to the Monk, you may retire, I shall give you a good Account of the *Depositum* you entrust me with. Upon this the Monk left us; I thanked him for his Kindness with a timorous Voice; for I was greatly troubled; and we went immediately into the Coach, my Benefactor and I.

I wish I could tell you all that passed in my Mind, and how much I was affected by this Conversation, of which I have told you but a very small part. For there passed between them several other disagreeable Hints about me; and it may not be improper to tell you, that as young as I was, my Temper inclined me towards being a little lofty. As I had been brought up with a tender Indulgence, and even with great Regard, a Conversation of that kind could not but shock me very much. Men's Favours are attended surely with an Aukwardness extremely mortifying to those who are to receive them. You must know, they had for an Hour together run through every little Particular of my Misery, so that their only Topick was the Compassion I had raised in them; and how meritorious it would be to do me good; and then, that Religion required

them

them to take Care of me. After which
followed a Crowd of proud, tho' charitable
Reflections, and all the emphatick Sentiments of an elated Devotion. In fhort,
Charity never made a more Pharifaical and
more ftately Parade of its melancholy Duties. My Heart was overwhelmed with
Shame at their devout Pageantry; and fince
I am upon that Subject, I muft tell you,
that nothing is more cruel than to depend
on the Help of a certain fort of People.
For what is Charity when it keeps no Mea-
fures towards the Miferable, and when it
never relieves a Soul, till it has wounded it
in the tendereft Part? A pretty Virtue,
indeed! which throws into Defpair thofe
who are the Objects of it. Pray is a Man
always charitable, for doing charitable
Actions? Very far from it. I might fay
to thofe Pretenders to Charity; when you
fo unmercifully infift on a particular Enu-
meration of my bad Circumftances; when
you bring me Face to Face with the whole
Group of my Misfortunes; when the Ce-
remonial of your mortifying Inquiries, or
rather of your burdenfome Examination
precedes the Affiftance you afford me, you
call that Charity; but I fay, it is a bru-
tifh, barbarous and hateful Action, a
meer Trade, and not the Refult of ge-
nuine Charity.

I have

I have now done. Let such as want any Information on that Head make their best Advantages of this. They may be sure I had it from the best Hand, since I speak by my own Experience.

To return, I was in the Coach, going to the Draper's with my Gentleman, and I remember very well, that he was much more inquisitive as we went, than he had been with the Monk, and that I answered him in a low dejected Voice. I durst hardly stir, and took up very little Room; for alas! I was like one dead.

However notwithstanding the deep Melancholy and Heaviness of my Heart, I was surprised at the Things he told me. Methought, his Conversation was pretty odd, and that his Stile grew milder on a sudden; that he was more fawning than zealous, and more generous than charitable, in short, quite another Man.

‘ You seem pretty much under Restraint
‘ with me, said he. I don't like to see you
‘ so reserved. It is what would soon grow
‘ into an Aversion for me, though I wish
‘ you more Good than any Man living.
‘ No doubt but our Conversation with the
‘ Monk has thrown you into this melan-
‘ choly Way. People of his Sort have a
‘ rough uncomfortable Way of expressing
‘ their Zeal, and we are sometimes forced
‘ in a manner to imitate them. But for my

2   ‘ part

' pert I am naturally tender-hearted;
' therefore, my dear Child, you may look
' upon me as your affured Friend, and
' one who has an hearty Concern for you,
' and defires you would repofe an intire
' Confidence in him, Do you hear? The
' only Right I fhall claim over you is, that
' of giving you now and then my Advice.
' Which I defire may not keep you at any
' diftance. Suppofe, for Inftance, I fhould
' tell you, that you are young and hand-
' fome, and that thefe two fine Endow-
' ments will expofe you to the amorous
' Addreffes of every giddy-brain'd Beau,
' that may chance to fee you; and that it
' would be very wrong to hearken to their
' Nonfenfe, becaufe it would be of no Ser-
' vice to you, and not worth your Atten-
' tion, which now muft be intirely bent on
' every thing that can raife your Fortune.
' I am not ignorant, that young Women
' of your Age are inchanted with the
' Thoughts of pleafing every Beholder.
' And I doubt not, but you will be uni-
' verfally admired, without any feeking of
' yours. But never make it your Bufinefs
' to pleafe every one, efpecially a thou-
' fand pert little Fellows, which your Si-
' tuation will require you not to mind.
' What I tell you does not proceed from
' any Excefs of Severity in me,' continued he, freely taking me by the Hand,
                                    which

which was none of the uglieſt. No, Sir, ſaid I. And then obſerving that I had no Gloves, I will buy you ſome, ſaid he; they preſerve the Hands, and that is worth the minding, when they happen to be hand-ſome.

Upon which he bid the Coachman ſtop; and he bought ſeveral Pair for me, all which I tried with his Aſſiſtance: For he would by all means help me, and I let him do ſo, always bluſhing at my Obedience; though I knew not why, and meerly by a kind of Inſtinct, which made me uneaſy and doubt-ful, what this might ſignifie.

All theſe little Particulars I mention to you, becauſe they really are not ſo inſigni-ficant as might be thought at firſt ſight.

At laſt, we arrived at the Draper's, who ſeemed to me a very good ſort of a Wo-man, and who received me on the Terms then agreed on for my Board. If I remem-ber well, he talked to her a good while in private. But I then apprehended nothing of what they had been ſaying. He went a-way at laſt, ſaying, that he ſhould come and viſit us ſoon; and recommended me very earneſtly to the Gentlewoman, who after he was gone, ſhewed me a little Room, wherein I put all my Things, and where I was to lye with another Woman.

I muſt, for the ſake of the Story, ac-quaint you with the Name of this Dealer. They

They called her Mrs. *Du Tour*, she was a Widow, and did not seem to be above Thirty: A fat jolly Woman, and who at first Sight might be taken for the best natured Creature in the World, and so she was. Her Family consisted of a little Boy her Son, of six or seven Years old, of a Maid, and one Mrs. *Toinon* her Journey-Woman.

Had the most unforeseen Accident happened to me, I could never have been more chagrined than I was in that House. Sensible People are much more and sooner cast down, on some Occasions, than others, because all that happens to them presently strikes to their very Heart. A certain stupid Melancholy invades them, with which I was seized myself: Mrs. *Du Tour* did all she could to force me out of that dismal State of Mind.

'Come, come, Mrs. *Marianne*, said she; (for she had asked my Name:) You are with very good-natured People. Pray don't be so melancholy. I love to see People merry. What ails you? Don't you like our Company? For my part, I no sooner saw you, but took a Fancy to you. There is our *Toinon*, who is a very good Girl, you must get acquainted with one another.' And all this she told me as we were at Supper. To which I made no Answer but with

an

an Inclination of my Head, and a Look that
thanked her for me. Sometimes I had
Courage enough to tell her, *Madam, you
are very kind.* But really I was there out
of my true Sphere, and born for quite o-
ther Company.

Methought there was fomething in the
blunt Sincerity of that Woman, which I
could not help being fhocked at. However, I never had lived before in any other
Company but that of the Vicar and his
Sifter, which were very far from being
People of the *Beau Monde.* 'Tis true,
their Ways were perfectly plain; but I never had obferved the leaft Rudenefs in them.
Their Difcourfes were unaffected, and full
of good Senfe. Honeft People of a mid-
dling Fortune might very well have fpo-
ken as they did. And had I never feen any
other Company, I fhould never have imagined there had been any better. Whereas
I could not be fatisfied in the leaft with
this Family. Their Language appeared to
me like a fort of Jargon or Gibberifh,
whofe Harfhnefs and Rafhnefs offended
the Nicety of my Ears. I was already
perfuaded, that in the *Beau Monde* there
was fomething much fuperior to this. I
longed mightily for that, and was very
forry to fee myfelf thus deprived of that
better Condition, to which I was as yet a
Stranger. Pray tell me whence do you
think

think this Turn of Mind might proceed?
Where had I contracted this Delicacy?
Did it run in my Blood? Possibly it might.
Or did it rather proceed from my having
lived a small time at *Paris?* Nor is that
unlikely.   There are penetrating Spirits
with whom a short Instruction has the Effect of a long Information; and who, from
the little they see, presently imagine all that
might be shewn to them.

Mine, I assure you, had a very piercing
and quick Apprehension; especially in
Things within its Sphere, such as the
World was.   I had no Acquaintance at
Paris, and knew very few of its Streets.
But there were in those Streets People of
all Kinds, and Coaches, and in those
Coaches a Species quite new, but not at all
strange to me.   And no doubt but there
was within me a natural Inclination, which
wanted nothing but these Objects to ex-
ert itself upon.   So that when I saw them,
it was just as if I had met with something
I looked for.

You may easily judge, that with such
Dispositions, neither Mrs. *Du Tour,* nor
Mrs. *Toinon* were fit Company for me.
The latter was a tall lusty Body, very strict
in holding back her Head.   She handled
her Shop-Goods with all the Judgment
and Address imaginable.   In which her
whole Soul was employed: For her Wit
was no longer than her Ell.   For

For my part, I was fo aukward at that
Bufinefs, that I provoked her Spleen every
Moment.   But then you fhould have feen
with what an Air of Conceitednefs and Self-
fufficiency fhe ufed to check me, and blame
my Want of Skill.   But the Jeft was,
that generally her Reprimands made me
ftill more aukward, becaufe my Difguft
was increafed by them.

We lay in the fame Room, as I told you
already, where fhe ufed to give me her Advice about arriving at Preferment, which
was her ufual Phrafe   And then fhe gave
an Account of her Relations; their Circumftances and Characters, told me what they
had given her the laft Year for her New-
Year's Gift.   Then fhe told me of her Lover, which was an handfome genteel Spark,
with whom we were to go out a walking
fome time or other.   To which I replied,
with all my Heart, though I had no great
Mind to it. She did not forget to mention
Mrs. *Du Tour*'s Sweet-heart, whom fhe
fhould already have made happy, but that
he was not rich enough, though he ufed
vifit her often, and eat with her ; and that
fhe made much of him,   I tell you all this
fine Stuff only to divert you.   If it tires
you, you may fkip it.

Mr. *De Climal*, (for that was the Name
of the Gentleman who had brought me to
Mrs. *Du Tour*) came again three or four

Days

Days after he had left me there.   I was
then in our Room with Mrs. *Toinon*, who
was very bufy about fhewing me her fine
Clothes, and who, out of Politenefs, left
the Room as foon as he came in.

Well, my dear Child! faid he, how do
you like your prefent Station? I hope,
anfwered I, that I fhall become ufed to it.
I fhould be very glad, faid he, to fee you
eafy; for I love you with all my Heart.
You pleafed me extremely the firft Moment I faw you; of which I fhall give you
as many convincing Proofs as fhall lie in
my Power.   Poor Dear! What a vaft Satisfaction I fhall find, in doing you Service!
But I muft have your Friendfhip in return.
I fhould be the moft ungrateful Creature
in the World, anfwered I, not to have a
true Friendfhip for you.   No, no, faid he,
it won't be for want of Gratitude you
don't love me; but becaufe you won't take
the Freedom with me, that I could wifh.
I am too fenfible of the Duty I owe you,
faid I; Nay, faid he, it is a Doubt whether you owe me any, fince we are uncertain who you are. But, *Marianne*, added
he, laying hold of my Hand, which he
fqueezed gently, would you not be a little
more familiar with a Friend, that would
wifh you fo well as I do? It is what I hope
from you. You would doubtlefs unveil all
your Sentiments and Inclinations to fuch a
Friend,

Friend, and be defirous to fee him often.
And why fhould you not be thus to me?
I muft have my Will in this, do you fee,
Child, or elfe we fhall have a hot Quarrel.
But hearkee, I had like to have forgot to
give you fome Money. And at the fame
time he put a few *Louidors* in my Hand.
At firft I refufed them, telling him, that I
had fomething left of the Deceafed's Money. But he neverthelefs forced me to accept of them. I took the Money, though with
a fort of Confufion. For there was fomething difguftful in it. But it was not then
neceffary for me to indulge my natural
Pride in that Point, efpecially with a Man
who had taken the Charge of me as a poor
Orphan, to whom he feemed refolved to
be as a Father.

When I received this Prefent I made him
a Courtefy with a grave Face. Ah! my
dear *Marianne*, faid he, no more of thefe
Courtefies. Shew me rather that you are
pleafed. Come, let us fee how many more
Courtefies you will make me for a whole
new Suit which I am going to give you. I
did not much mind the Suit he promifed
me ; but he faid this with fuch a feeming
good Nature, and fo much Humour, that I
muft own he won my Heart entirely. All
my Reluctancies vanifhed on a fudden, and
were fucceeded by the quickeft Senfe of
Gratitude. I threw myfelf on his Arm,
which

which I kiffed very gracefully, and was ready to cry, I was fo affected by it.

He was ravifhed to fee this fudden Motion, and took and kiffed my Hand very poffionately ; a manner of acting which, even in the Hurry of my little Tranfport, appeared to me odd and fingular enough, but ftill of that fort of Singularity which furprifed me, without opening my Eyes, or difcovering his real Sentiments, and which I was inclined to take for a quick though pretty uncommon Expreffion of his good Nature.

However, from that inftant the Converfation began to be freer on my Side. My eafy Ways gave me Charms, which he was not yet acquainted with. He fometimes ftood motionlefs, gazing on me with a Tendernefs, which I always obferved to be extraordinary, without apprehending what it meant.

And indeed I could then by no means penetrate any further into his Defigns : For my Imagination had already fixed my Ideas, with regard to that Man. Though I faw him inchanted with me, yet I thought my Youth, Circumftances, Wit and Beauty, might poffibly have infpired him, with a very innocent Affection for me. Men are apt to conceive a Tendernefs for young Girls of my Age, of whom they are refolved to take Care. They are extremely

D   pleafed

pleafed to fee them have Merit, becaufe their Favours to them will turn more to their Honour. In fhort, we generally like to fee the Objects of our Generofity; and a Girl of fifteen and a half, though fhe have no great Experience, may neverthelefs eafily guefs at all the tender Motives of her Benefactor in fuch a Cafe. She is no more furprifed at them, than fhe would be at her Father's or her Mother's Fondnefs for her. And that was exactly the Opinion I had of this Perfon. I fhould much fooner have taken him for an Original, and one whofe Ways were odd and fingular, than for what he really was. He took my Hand a thoufand Times and kiffed it as it were in jeft: The only thing I admired in this was the hafty Progrefs of his Inclination for me; a Thought which affected me more than all his Favours.

It would perhaps be much better not to mention all thefe little Particulars; but I write as well as I can. I muft not think that I am now making a Book, for that would difcompofe my Mind too much. I rather chufe to fancy myfelf converfing with you, becaufe what paffes in Converfation is tolerable. Let us then proceed.

Women in thofe Days dreffed in their Hair. None could have finer Locks than mine; and even now, though my Years have diminifhed their Number, the Colour

lour

lour of them is not at all altered, for they are still of the finest light Chesnut.

Mr. *De Climal* looked at them and handled them with Passion. But I took this as a meer Frolick. *Marianne*, said he sometimes, I don't think you very ill provided indeed; for such fine Hair and such a handsome Face will never let you want any thing. They never will restore my Parents, answer'd I. 'Tis true, said he, but they will make every Body love you, and for my Part, I never shall refuse them any Thing. I make no Doubt of that, Sir, I replied; I depend intirely on you and your tender Heart. Ah! my dear Child, said he, do you talk of a Heart? Would you then give me yours if I asked it? Indeed you deserve it richly, replied I, with an unthinking Ingenuity.

The Words were scarce out of my Mouth, but I saw his Eyes sparkling, and so full of Fire, that they like a sudden Flash of Lightning forced me to open my Eyes. I immediately reflected, that it might be possible this Man might love me as a Mistress. For I had seen Lovers in the Country. I had heard them talk of Love, and even had read some Romances privately. All which, together with what Nature teaches us, had made me sensible at least, that a Lover is very different from a Friend. And from that Difference, which I had

framed

framed to myself, Mr. *De Climal*'s Glances began to appear very suspicious.

However, I did not take this sudden Suspicion for an unquestionable Certainty; but resolved not to be very long dubious of the Matter. In the mean time, I began to be a little more free and easy with him. My Conjectures freed me almost intirely of that Bashfulness he so often reproached in me. I thought that in case he were truly in Love with me, I had no more Occasion to be so ceremonious with him, and that it was He, not I, whose Mind ought to be perplexed Nature it self taught me to argue thus. The Argument might perhaps be thought to proceed from much Cunning; whereas nothing can be imagined more simple. Nor do those that make it even know that they do so.

'Tis true, the Men against whom we Reason after this manner, have no great Returns to hope for from us. For it inti mates, that in Point of Love we care but very little for them. And indeed Mr. *De Climal* was perfectly indifferent to me in this respect, and my Indifference for him was even such, that the least Provocation would have changed it into Hatred. Perhaps he might have been my first Inclination, had our Acquaintance began in another manner. But I never knew him but

upon

upon the footing of a very pious Gentleman whose Charity induced him to take Care of me. And I don't know any Way of becoming acquainted with People, less productive of what we call Love. He that has had that kind of Intercourse with one, cannot hope by any Means to raise a Woman's Affection. For the Mortification she has therein undergone, has effectually stopped all the Avenues of her Heart. The Heart as it were repines, even insensibly to itself, so long as you require no other Sentiments of it, but those which are of right yours. But if you expect from it another sort of Affection, the Case is quite altered; for then Self-love revives and knows you perfectly well. It is on that Occasion your irretrievable Enemy, with whom no Peace is to be hoped. And this was exactly my Disposition with regard to Mr. *De Climal.*

I really believe that if Men knew but how to oblige others, they might expect every thing from them. For can any thing be more agreeable to the Mind, than a true Sense of Gratitude, when our Self-love is not against it? Sure, that would be an inexhaustible Source of Tenderness. Whereas two great Virtues are necessary with Men; the one to hinder us from being filled with Indignation and even Disgust at their Favours towards us, and the other to oblige us to be grateful for them.

Mr. *De Climal* had told me of a Suit of Clothes he intended to give me, and we went together, to buy it according to my Fancy. I believe I should have refused it, had I been fully convinced of his being in Love with me. For methinks I should then have the greatest Reluctance to the making any Advantage of his Weakness, especially because I did not share it with him; for in those Cases, when Love is mutual, we adjust all Matters; and fancy, that the highest Degreee of Delicacy consists on such Occasions in silencing our Scruples. But I was still uncertain of the inward Sentiments of this Man. And in Case they should be nothing but Friendship, I concluded, that it must needs be Friendship in the highest Degree, and consequently that I could do no less in return than shake off all manner of Pride towards him. Therefore I accepted of his Present at all Adventures.

The Clothes were bought. I chose them grave and handsome, and such as might have fitted a young Lady not over rich. Then Mr. *De Climal* talked of Linen; and I really wanted some. This was another Purchase we made at the same time. Mrs. *Du Tour* might very well have sold us that Linen, but he had good Rea-

fons

fons for his not buying it of her. For he would needs give me fome of the fineft, and Mrs. *Du Tour* would certainly have thought it an Excefs of Charity. And though fhe was a good plain Creature, which would never have examined the Cafe too clofely, becaufe fhe would have judged it was no Bufinefs of her's, he thought it much properer, not to truft her Plainnefs on this Occafion, and to go fome where elfe.

I was forced at laft to open my Eyes, for this fine Linen left me no room in the leaft to doubt of the Nature of his Sentiments. I even wondered how the Clothes, which were alfo very fine, had not fhewn me plainly what his Motive was. For Charity is not gallant in her Liberalities, and even Friendfhip itfelf, though always fo ready to afford Help, gives what is good and fubftantial, and never offers what is magnificent. The Virtues of Men never do more than their Duties, and therein chufe rather to be fparing than profufe. Vices alone know no Bounds. I whifpered him in his Ear, that I would never accept of Linen fo coftly and magnificent. And I was very ferious and earneft when I fpoke it. But he laughed at me, and faid; Hold your Tongue, Huzzy, you are a Child and a Fool; go to your Glafs and fee whether this Linen is too fine for your

Face;

Face; and then went on, without minding what I said.

I muſt own that this puzzled me extremely. For then I ſaw plainly he was in Love with me. That his Generoſity had no other Motive than that he hoped thereby to gain my Affection, and that I gave him very great reaſon to hope for it, by accepting his Preſents.

I then was adviſing with myſelf what to do. And at this time, now I think cooly of it, I really believe, that I conſulted only to loſe time. I made a thouſand different Reflections, and ſo made Work for my ſelf, that in the Diſorder and Confuſion of my Thoughts, I might be the leſs able to take my Reſolutions, and that my Suſpence might be more excuſable. By which means I defered my Rupture with Mr. *De Climal*, and conſequently kept his fine Preſents.

However, I was very much aſhamed of his Deſigns. My dear Friend the Vicar's Siſter came into my Mind again. What an immenſe Difference, ſaid I to myſelf, is there between the Help ſhe afforded me and that I now receive! How violent, how afflicting would it be to that dear Creature, if ſhe was alive, to ſee me in this Condition! Methought this laſt Adventure was a barbarous, and even a ſacrilegious Violation of the great Regard and

Ten-

Tenderneſs I ought to have kept for her Memory. Nay, methought her Heart was ſighing bitterly within mine, and reproaching me for my exceſſive Weakneſs. The Senſe of it I very ſeverely felt, but to deſcribe it would never have been in my Power.

On the other Hand: I had no Place to be in; and Mr. *De Climal* had procured me one. I had no Clothes; and he bought me ſome. Beſides they were of the beſt Sort, and I had already tried them in my Fancy, and found that they fitted me to a Nicety. But I was reſolved not to inſiſt on that Head, becauſe the great Pleaſure it would have cauſed me, would at the ſame time have made me bluſh: And very likely I was glad to indulge that pleaſing Idea, without being myſelf Accomplice. A wonderful Artifice indeed! to avoid the Guilt of a Fault we have a Mind to commit! And then I continued to argue thus with myſelf. Mr. *De Climal* has not yet made a Declaration of his Love, and perhaps will not venture to do it yet a great while. It is no Buſineſs of mine, to gueſs at the Motives of his Care for me. I have been introduced to him, as a pious charitable Man, and it is in that Quality he is ſo beneficial to me. If he does it with a bad Deſign, ſo much the worſe for him. I am not obliged to dive into his Heart, and

I ſhall

I fhall be the Accomplice of none of his Faults, fo long as he fhall not be plain with me. Therefore it will be time enough to refufe his Prefents, when he fpeaks to me without Difguife.

This little Cafe of Confcience thus refolved, all my Scruples vanifhed, and I thought the Linen and Clothes were very lawfully mine.

I took them to Mrs. *Du Tour*'s, and in our way Home, Mr. *De Climal* made now and then his Paffion a little more evident than ufual. He unmafked by degrees, and the Lover infenfibly took Place of the Devotee. I could already fee half of his Face: But I was refolved, not to feem to know him, before he would fhew the whole, and to be perfectly blind till then. The fine Clothes were not yet fecured, and I had perhaps loft them, by being fcrupulous too foon. Perfons haraffed by fuch Paffions, as that Mr. *De Climal* had for me, are naturally bafe, ungenerous and fhamelefs, when abfolutely difappointed. They don't much value the making an handfome and honourable Retreat: And he is a very odious and a defpicable Lover, who is more for poffeffing the Perfon than the Inclinations of his Miftrefs. Not that the moft delicate Lovers have no Defires; But at leaft the Sentiments of their Hearts go Hand in Hand with the Gratification of their Senfes, and this Mixture

ture conftitutes a tender not a vicious Love,
liable however to degenerate into it.   For
in Point of Love, there are every Day very
grofs Actions done, under the Notion, of
great Delicacy.   But this is not the Point.

I then made as if I did not underftand
the fawning Expreffions Mr. *De Climal*
ufed in our Way to Mrs. *Du Tour*'s.   *Marianne*, faid he, I am afraid I fhall love
you too much: But if the Thing fhould
happen, what would you then do?   All
I could do, anfwered I, fhould be to become ftill more grateful, if fo be, my Gratitude can poffibly increafe.   Neverthelefs,
faid he, my dear *Marianne*, I pretty much
doubt what your Heart will do, when it
is once informed of all the Tendernefs I
have for you.   For you are very far from
knowing how great it is.   How! faid I,
you believe then that I am not fenfible of
your Friendfhip? Ah! faid he, pray don't
change my Expreffions; I don't fay **my**
Friendfhip, I fpeak of my Tendernefs.
Why! faid I, is it not the fame Thing? No
Marianne, replied he, looking at me with an
Air that fhould immediately have fhewn me
that Difference; No, dear Child! it is not
the fame thing; and I fhould be overjoy'd to
fee you more pleafed and more delighted
with the one, than the other.   At this Difcourfe I could not help cafting down my
Eyes, though I ftrove not to do it; but the

grea**t**

great Lofs I was at quite over-powered me.
You anfwer nothing, faid he? Did you
then comprehend me at laft, added he,
fqueezing my Hand? It is, faid I, becaufe I am afhamed to find myfelf not able
to anfwer all your Kindneffes.

By good Luck, our Converfation end-
ed there, for we were juft at Home. All
he could do was to whifper thefe Words
in my Ear. Go, you Huzzy, you dear
Rogue! Go and make your Heart a little
lefs hard and more apprehenfive, I leave
mine with you to help on the Work.

This Difcourfe was pretty plain, nor
could a Man well fpeak more intelligibly.
I made as if I took no Notice, that I
might not be obliged to give him an
Anfwer. But I was at laft forced, whether I would or not, to mind a Kifs he gave
my Ear, as he was fpeaking, and to break
Silence, which I did thus. Pray, Sir, faid
I to him in an innocent manner, and as if
I took his Kifs for a Jogg of his Head a-
gainft mine, did not I hurt you? Juft as
I was faying thefe Words, I came out of
the Coach, and I really think he was du-
ped, by my little Artifice, for he anfwered me very naturally, No.

I took the Bundle, and went to lock it
up in my Room, while Mr. *De Climal*
ftood in Mrs. *Du Tour*'s Shop. I was down
again immediately. *Marianne,* faid he to
me

me in a grave Tone, order your Clothes to be gone about to Day: I shall see you again in three or four Days, when I would have you wear them. And then addressing himself to Mrs. *Du Tour* ; I endeavoured, said he, to buy the Clothes suitable to a Number of very fine Shifts she shewed me, that were left to her by the Gentlewoman, that is dead.

And you must know that Mr. *De Climal* had told me before-hand, that he should give the Thing that Turn to Mrs *Du Tour*. I believe I have already hinted the Reason he had for so doing, though he had said nothing to me. But I guessed so. Besides, added he, speaking still to Mrs. *Du Tour*, I think it proper, that Mrs. *Marianne* be handsomely dressed, because I have a Prospect for her, that may possibly succeed. And all this he said in the manner of a worthy and reputable Man. For Mr. *De Climal*, alone with me, did not in the least resemble Mr. *De Climal* conversing with others. Really they were two very different Persons. And when I saw him with his devout Looks, I could not conceive how that grave and venerable Countenance could possibly become profane, and be so altered as it appeared to me. Blest Heaven! How many Talents have Men, to make them good for nothing!

He retired after he had talked about half

a quarter of an Hour with Mrs. *Du Tour*.
He no fooner was gone but this Perfon, to
whom he had given my Hiftory, began to
cry up his Piety and Good Nature. *Marianne*, faid fhe, you had indeed extraordinary good Luck, when you got acquainted
with him. For you fee he takes as much
Care of you as if you were his own Child.
I very much doubt whether the Gentleman
has his Fellow in the World, either for
Goodnefs orCharity.

I did not much relifh that laft Word,
which was a little too plain and downright for
one whofe Self-love was fo tender as mine.
But Mrs. *Du Tour* knew no better. Her
Expreffions were agreeable to her Underftanding, which was in Proportion to her
want of Art and Cunning. Neverthelefs
it made me look four. However I held
my Tongue, for we had no Witnefs of our
Converfation fave the grave and ferious
Mrs. *Toinon*, who was much readier to envy my fine Clothes, than to think me in
any fort humbled by receiving them. Indeed Mrs. *Marianne*, faid fhe to me with
fomething of a jealous Air, fure you were
wrapt in your Mother's Smock, you were
born to fuch a good Fortune. Quite the
contrary, faid I, I am born to be very unfortunate; for, were things as they fhould
be, I ought to be without Comparifon
much better than I am. *A propos*, faid
she;

ſhe; is it true that you have neither Father nor Mother, nor any other Relation? That is comical. Very comical indeed! ſaid I in an angry Tone: I wonder Mrs. *Toinon*, you did not congratulate me upon it. Hold your Tongue, you Fool, ſaid Mrs. *Du Tour*, who ſaw I was vexed; ſhe is in the right to laugh at you. Should you not rather thank God, for having kept you your Parents? Was ever any Thing more ſtupid, than to tell People, that they were Foundlings. I had as live be called a Baſtard.

Pray was not this a very comfortable Way of taking my Part? But then the Zeal of this good Body ſhocked me as much as the Impertinence of the other, ſo that I could not forbear crying. This moved Mrs. *Du Tour* much, who never ſuſpected it was owing to her Silliness. Her Concern for me made me dread ſome new Reprimands from *Toinon*, and I forthwith begged her to let that Subject drop.

Toinon on her Part ſeeing me cry, was really quite diſconcerted; for ſhe was an harmleſs Creature alſo, and had no Intention to vex any Body. Only ſhe was vain, becauſe ſhe thought it very becoming. But not having a new Suit of Clothes as well as I, ſhe thought perhaps it was proper to make Amends for it, by ſaying ſomething witty, and to raiſe her Wit as ſhe uſe to do her Head. This

This gave Birth to the fine Compliment she made me, for which she very sincerely begged my Pardon. As I saw that these good harmless plain Creatures had no Notion at all of my Kind of Pride; that my Niceties were downright Hebrew to them, and that they did not suspect the least Part of the Trouble they had occasioned me; I was presently appeased by their good Words, and my Clothes were at last the only Thing minded. The eager Curiosity they had to see them, made me curious too, to hear what they thought of them.

I then went up to fetch them without the least Grudge, not a little overjoyed at the Thoughts, that I should soon wear them. I took the Bundle, just as it was when I carried it up, and down I brought it. I opened it, and what should we see first, but the fine Linen, the Purchase we had taken so much Pains to conceal, and which had cost Mr. *de Climal* the contriving of a Story and me the consenting to it. How giddy are young Brains! I had forgot, that this nasty Linen was in the Bundel with the Clothes. Oh! oh! said Mrs. *Du Tour*, there is something new. Mr. *De Climal* told us that your deceased Friend had left you that, though he bought it for you. Fy, *Marianne*, that is very wrong done on you, not to have had it of me. Pray, are you more nice than our

Dutchesses,

Dutcheffes, who buy their Linen of us?
And your Mr. *De Climal*, I think, is
very comical. But I fee very well what
it is, faid fhe, reaching at the Stuff of my
Clothes, which was under the Linen, to
fee it; (For her Anger did not put a Stop
to her Curiofity; And Curiofity, you
know, is a Motion in Women which attends every Thing they have in their Head.)
I fee, I fee what it is, faid fhe, I eafily
guefs the Reafon why Mr. *De Climal* had
a Mind to impofe on me with Regard to
that Linen; But— I am not fo ftupid as he
might take me to be: Well, well——,I fhall
fay no more, but—, Away, away with your
fine Linen. Upon my Word 'tis a very
clever Trick ! Mr. *De Climal* is kind enough
to bring me Mrs. *Marianne* as a *Boarder*; but
what fhe wants he goes to another Shop for.
I am to have all the Trouble and other
People all the Benefit; I affure you !——

During all this, *Toinon* handled my Stuff
with the Tip of her Fingers, as if fhe had
been afraid of dirtying them. Good lack-
a-day ! faid fhe, fee what it is to be an Orphan ! And this fhe faid only to have a
Part in the Scene: For the poor Soul, as
honeft and virtuous as fhe was, would have
been pleafed down to the Ground, had any
Man made her a Prefent of the fame Kind.
Let that alone, faid Mrs, *Du Tour* to her;
I hope you are not jealous of fuch a Job
as this.
                                    Hitherto

Hithefto I had been filent ; for I was fo confufed, fo vexed, arid agitated by fo many violent Paffions at once, that I knew not how to begin. Befides, it was a very ftrange and new Situation to me, to fee myfelf in fuch a Scuffle as this. I never had feen the like in my Life. At laft, when my Confufion was a little over, Anger got the better. But it was fuch a true and undiffembled Rage, that none could have been tranfported with the like, but one that was perfectly innocent of what this Woman hinted at.

Nor was it lefs true, that Mr. *De Climal* was in Love with me. But I knew very well, that my Intention was, never to make the leaft Advantage of it. And if I had accepted of his Prefents knowing his Paffion, I had done it at the Inftigation of a little deceitful Argument, which my Wants and Vanity infpired me with, and which had not in the leaft altered the perfect Integrity of my Intentions. My Way of reafoning, no doubt, was wrong ; but 'twas no Crime ; therefore I did not deferve the outrageous Infinuations with which Mrs. *Du Tour* had afperfed me. But then I made fuch an Uproar that the whole Houfe rung again with it. I firft threw the Linnen and Clothes on the Ground, not for any Reafon, but purely out of Paffion and Fury. I talked then at Random and

and roared out. 'Tis impoſſible to tell you all I ſaid in my Rage and Deſpair. Only I remember, that I owned with many Tears, that Mr. *De Climal* had bought the Linen, and bid me not to tell it, without giving me the Reaſon why. And that as for the reſt, I thought my ſelf very unfortunate to be with People ſo very ready to accuſe me raſhly ; That I would leave the Houſe immediately, and ſend for a Coach to carry away my Things : That I would go at all Adventures, and that it was much better for ſuch a Girl as I was to die, than to live ſo much out of her own Sphere ; and that I would leave them Mr. *De Climal*'s Preſents, which I did not care a Pin for, any more than I did for his Love, in Caſe he had any for me. In ſhort, I was like a little Tyger. My Brains were quite turned. Beſides, every Thing that could aggravate me, preſented itſelf to my Imagination at the ſame Time. The Death of my dear good Friend : My being for ever deprived of her Tenderneſs : The fatal Loſs of my Parents : All the Mortifications I had already undergone : The diſmal frightful Thought of being a Stranger to all the World, and of not having the leaſt Hint of my Extraction : The Proſpect of my Miſery, which perhaps might have no other End but a ſtill greater Diſaſter : (For my Beauty was then the only Thing

that

that could procure me any Friends; And
Lord! what a pitiful Refuge is the Vices
of Mankind!) Pray, were not all these
Things together enough to overturn such a
young Brain as mine?

Mrs. *Du Tour* was frighten'd to see me in
such a violent Transport; For she never
thought I could be capable of it, and only
expected to see me out of Countenance.
Lord! *Marianne*, said she to me, when
she could find Room to bring in a Word,
any Body may be deceived; Pray, Child,
moderate your Passion a little; I am sorry
for what I have said: (For my excessive
Rage did evidently justify me in her Opinion, it being too keen, to proceed from
a guilty Conscience.) Come, come, Child,
said she, be satisfied: But I did not give
over for all she could say, and would by
all means be gone.

At last, she pushed me into a little Par-
lour, where she lock'd herself up with me,
and there I went on with such an Eager-
ness, that it exhausted my whole Strength.
I was perfectly out of Breath, and could
no longer express my excessive Grief, but
by crying, which I did most desperately,
and the good Mrs. *Du Tour* seeing this began also to cry very heartily.

Upon this, *Toinon* came in to tell us
Dinner was ready, and as she was always
of every Body's Opinion, she cried for
Com-

Company ; and I, after this Flood of Tears, being moved at laſt by all their mild Words and Careſſes, ſuffered my Paſſion to abate. I quickly cheared up, and all was forgot.

Perhaps the good Rate Mr. *De Climal* paid for my Board, contributed ſomething to the tender Regret Mrs. *Du Tour* expreſſed of having vexed me : Juſt as ſhe had been much more ſet againſt me for her not having ſold the Linnen than for any Thing elſe : For during Dinner-Time having quite altered her Style, ſhe told me herſelf, that if Mr. *De Climal* did really love me, as he ſeemed to do, I ought to make the beſt Advantage of it. (Lord! I ſhall never forget her Words as long as I live) Heark ye, *Marianne*, ſaid ſhe, were I in your Place I know very well what I would do. For ſince you are diſmal poor, and deſtitute of all Comfort, even of that of Parents, I would firſt of all take whatever Mr. *De Climal* ſhould give me, and make as great an Advantage that Way as I could. Nor ſhould I love him a bit the more for that ; I would be hang'd firſt : For Honour muſt go before any Thing elſe, and I am not the Woman that would ſay otherwiſe, as you ſaw very well. In a Word, do what you pleaſe you will always find that nothing is more commendable than to be virutuous, and I ſhall die

in

in that Opinion. But that does not argue,
that we are obliged to throw away what
Good foever offers itfelf to us. Things in
Life may be reconciled. For Inftance,
you and Mr. *De Climal*; Well, muft you
bid him be gone? No, fure. He loves
you, 'tis true, but is that your Fault? All
your Bigots do the fame Thing. Let him
love you, if he pleafes, and let every one
anfwer for himfelf. Why! He buys you
Things? Well, take them, Child. Are
they not paid for? If he gives you Money,
don't be filly, but accept on't freely. For
your Part is not to be ftiff and proud. If
he afks you to love him? Softly for that.
You muft play cunning with him. Tell
him, that you don't love him; but that it
is not impoffible but in Time you might.
To give one's Word, and to retract it,
fometimes goes a great way. Firft you
muft get Time, to bring yourfelf to love
him: And then, when you make as if you
had begun, you will want Time to increafe
that Love: And when he fhall think you
ought to be intirely his, will not your Honour be a fufficient Excufe with him?
Muft not a Girl always put a Man off?
Has fhe not a thoufand good Reafons to
plead? Can't fhe for Inftance preach to
him, and make him fenfible of the Hei-
noufnefs of his Intentions? During all
which Time paffes, and you receive Prefents,

without

without asking for them. And if a Man
at last grows pert ; Why then, let him go
and be hanged. Cannot one be as angry
as he, and turn him off? But nevertheless,
what he has given is a Present. In Troth!
Nothing is prettier than Gift: and if there
were no Givers, People would keep all
they have to themselves. Upon my Word,
if any of your holy Folks had taken a
Fancy to me, and should pretend to court
me, I assure you he might make me Pre-
sents till Doom's Day, before I should bid
him stop.

The ingenuous and warm Zeal with
which Mrs. *Du Tour* uttered these fine Maxims, was still better than the Maxims
themselves, which are indeed something
remiss and indulgent; but which might
also make very strange Girls of Honour,
of such as would put her Instructions in
Practice. The Doctrine of them is a little
dangerous. I believe its Tendency is to
lead us to the Brink of Lewdness; and I
don't think it an easy Matter to remain
virtuous and honest in such a Road.

As young as I was, I did not in the least
approve of what she said. And really,
though a Girl were perfectly sure of
always keeping herself honest, the Practice of these unworthy Maxims would always be sufficient Matter of Shame and
Dishonour to her. And has she not actually

tually quitted all Honour, who gives the
leaft Handle to a Man to hope, that fhe
could poffibly lofe it? Nay, the vile Art
of keeping a Man in fuch Hopes is in my
Mind much more fhameful, than a total
abandoning of one's felf to Vice could be.
For of the moft infamous Bargains that
are made, the worft are thofe wherein Ava-
rice is the Inducement to be falfe and deceitful.   Pray, are you not of my Opinion?

For my Part, I was too true and fin-
cere ever to think of ufing thofe vile little
Tricks.   I would neither do ill, nor feem
capable of doing it.   Double-dealing of
all kinds was my Averfion.   But above
all I abhorred this, on Account of the
very great Bafenefs of its Motive.

I fhook my Head, therefore, at all the
fine Speeches, by which Mrs. *Du Tour*
endeavoured to change my Sentiments in
this Matter, for her own Advantage as well
as for mine.   She would have been very
glad, for her Part, if my Penfion had lafted
long, and if we had lived a little, and
junketed upon Mr. *De Climal's* Money.
For fhe gave me to underftand this in
jeft; for the good Woman loved good
eating, and was horridly covetous; whereas
I was neither.

When we had dined, my Clothes and
Linen were given to the Work-women,
whom

whom Mrs. *Du Tour* charged to make Dif-
patch. No doubt but fhe hoped, that
when I fhould once have feen my felf well
rigged and fpruce; (for thefe were her
Expreffions,) perhaps I might be tempted
to fpin out my Adventure with Mr. *De
Climal* a little longer, and to keep him a
while at Bay. And I muft own that in
Point of Vanity, I already gave very great
Hopes of being pretty much of a Woman.
A Ribbon well chofen, and a genteel Suit
of Clothes, whenever I met any, were fufficient to make me ftop fhort. My Fancy
glowed, at the Sight of them, and my Agi-
tation of Heart would continue for an Hour
after. I never ceafed, imagining myfelf
decked with all thofe Trifles, as I had
done by the Clothes Mr. *De Climal* had
bought me. In fhort my Fancy was always projecting fomething that way, till
I could come at the Realities.

But however, as I was no longer doubt-
ul of Mr. *De Climal's* Love, I was fully
refolved, in Cafe he fhould give me any
hint of it, to tell him that it would be
to no Purpofe; Which done, I might
take all his Prefents without any Scruple.
This was the whole Purport of my little
fcheme.

Four Days after my Clothes and Linen
were brought Home. It was on a Holiday, and they came juft as I got out of

E   Bed.

Bed. At the Sight of them, both *Toinon*
and I became ſtupiſied and ſpeechleſs; I
for Joy, and ſhe on Account of the great
Diſproportion that ſhe apprehended was
going to begin between her Appearance
and mine. She would then willingly have
exchanged her Parents for my Orphan
Condition, might ſhe but have been ſo well
dreſſed. She gazed on my little Equipage
with a Pair of ſtupid, ſtaring, jealous Eyes.
But her Envy had ſuch a Mixture of Hu
miliation in it, and ſhewed her to be ſo
very much mortified, that in the midſt of
my Tranſport I could not forbear pitying
her. But her Grief could not be helped;
And I, to ſpare her, tried my Clothes with
as great Humility as I could, before a little
impertinent looking Glaſs, which would
ſcarce give me a View of half my Perſon:
But how ſmart and killing was the half I
beheld in my own Eyes?

I then began to dreſs my Head as ſoon
as ever I could, to enjoy all my Ornaments
at once. My Heart went pit-a-pat, when
I but thought how pretty I was going to
be. Nay, that Thought even made my
Hand tremble every Pin I ſtuck. I made
as much Speed as I could; yet without be
ing over haſty: For I was reſolved every
Thing ſhould be done to Perfection: But
I had ſoon finiſhed; for the Perfection I
then knew in Point of Dreſs was not very

extensive. 'Tis true I began with wonderfully good Dispositions; but that was all.

But then you should have seen what a Work I have had in that Respect, since I knew more of the World. Men talk of their Sciences and Philosophy, and cry up their learned Stuff: But they are none of them to be compared to the important Skill of placing a Ribbon with Judgment, or of determining what Colour it should be of.

If one could but know what passes in a Coquet's Head, on such Occasions; if we could but observe, how penetrating, how sharp and delicate her Soul is in the Judgments she makes, on the Fashions she tries, rejects, hesitates, and at last pitches on, when weary of her Uncertainty and Irresolution: (For it frequently happens that she is dissatisfied; Her Performance always falling very short of what she intended ;) I say, if one could but know the vast Importance and endless Discussion of all those material Points; It would be enough to frighten even the most able Capacities; and *Aristotle* himself would be but a School-boy, compared to a Coquet. This I affirm, because I know it throughly. When in Matter of Dress you have once found out what is well, it is but a very indifferent Discovery: For you must find out what is better, in order to arrive at last at what is better still. And to at-tain that fuperlative Degree, you muft dive into the Souls of Men, that you may prefer what will pleafe them moft to what does only pleafe them much. And is not this the chief and moft extenfive of all Sciences?

You fee, I am a little jocular on our Arts of Coquetry. And why fhould I fcruple to do it now to you, fince the Time for exercifing that Art is over for either of us? And for my Part, if any Body would laugh at having feen me formerly a Coquet, let him come to me, and he fhall hear from me a thoufand coquetifh Tricks of mine perhaps, which he knows not yet, and then we fhall fee, who will have moft Caufe to laugh, he or I.

I have a roguifh little Face of my own, which has coft me many an extravagant Trick. Tho' one could never imagine by its prefent melancholy Form, that it ever deferved to have had fo much Trouble taken with it. But then I pity it, when I behold it: An Honour which I do it very feldom, and hardly ever on purpofe. But what makes amends for it is, That I indulged my Vanity formerly, more than any Woman ever did. I had all the Ways of making my felf agreeable at my Fingers Ends. I knew how to be feveral forts of Women in the fame Breath. When I wanted to put on a little pert Air, I had a certain Gesture and Dress, wherewith I was sure of Success. The very next Day you might have seen me with a tender languishing Countenance; and on a third I assumed a modest, serious, and a careless Look. I was sure of fixing the most unsteady Man, and of deceiving his Constancy, by changing, or rather every day metamorphosing his Mistress, which with regard to him was as much as if he had had a new one.

But I am always wandering from my Subject. Pray forgive my Digressions. They divert and even help me sometimes to a little Breath. Besides, you know I am now conversing with you.

I was then soon dress'd, and really I so perfectly eclipsed poor *Toinon*, that I was ashamed of it. I appeared an Angel in Mrs. *Du Tour*'s Eyes. But *Toinon* could not forbear finding Faults with my Clothes, and I approved of every`Thing she said out of meer Charity. For had I given Vent to all my Joy, her Mortification would have been much greater, and therefore I concealed it. My Heart, you must know, always inclined me to have those little Regards for that of others.

I was impatient to shew my self, and to go to Church, to see how much I should be looked at. *Toinon*, who had her Sweetheart with her every Holiday went out before me, for fear I should follow her, and

left

left in cafe we fhould go together he fhould
look at me more than at her, on Account
of my fine Clothes ; For a new Suit is with
fome People very near on a Level with an
handfome Face.

I then went out alone a little out of Countenance: Becaufe I fancied there was one
particular Look to be kept, and that my
Beauty and Attire required me to be more
than ordinary upon my Guard. I held up
my Head with great Care ; For that is the
beginning of an uninftructed Vanity ;
and as much as I can remember, I think I
refembled pretty much a young little lovely
frefh coloured Girl juft come from a Country Education, who cannot help being a
little aukward : But whofe Charms yet
imprifoned feem to ftrive to get abroad.

Nor did I make the beft of all the Charms
of my Face. I had abandoned that to its
own Conduct ; (as you faid very comically
the other Day, fpeaking of another Woman) Yet for all that I was much looked
at by feveral that paffed by. I was more
delighted than furprifed at this, for I was
fully fenfible it was no more than my Due.
And to tell you the Truth, there were but
very few Perfons fo compleat as mine. I
pleafed the Heart as much as the Eye, and
Beauty was the leaft of my Advantages.

Now I am entring upon an Event which
has been the original Caufe of all my other
                                    Adven-

Adventures, and I shall begin the second
Part of my Life with it.   For it would
doubtless tire you, if you was obliged to
read it all in a Breath, and a little Pause
will refresh us both.

The End of the first Part of *the* LIFE of
MARIANNE.

ADVERTISEMENT.

THE *first Part of the Life of* Marianne *has, it seems, been acceptable to many Persons, who among other Things have chiefly been delighted with the Reflections with which it is interspersed. Others again have thought the Number of these too great, and it is to such I address this short Preface.*

If an Author should offer them a Book intituled Reflections on Mankind, *would they not read it with Pleasure, if the Reflections were good? And, have we not Numbers of these Books, some of which are much valued? Why then should they be displeased with Reflections here, only because they are Reflections?*

But, say they, they are not in their proper Place, when mixed with Adventures like these, in which the Business is to amuse not to set us on thinking.

My Answer is; If you look upon Marianne's *Life as a Romance, you are certainly in the right. In that Case your Critick is just. There are then too many Reflections in it, and it has not the Form usually given to Romances, or Tales written only to amuse the Reader. But* Marianne *did not in the least intend to*

write

ADVERTISEMENT.

write a Romance. Her Friend asks her for the History of her Life, and she pens it in her own Manner. Marianne has no Scheme for making a Book. She is no Author, but only a thinking Woman, who has passed through a great Variety of Stations; who has seen much of the World, Whose Life in short is a Series of Events, which have given her a thorough Knowledge of the human Heart, and of Men's Characters. When she relates her Adventures, she fancies herself conversing with a Friend, to whom she speaks or answers in a familiar manner. And it is with that Disposition of Mind she without Distinction intersperses the Facts she relates, with the Reflections those Facts naturally raise in the Mind. This is what made Marianne write her Life in the Method she has done. Her Style, if you please, is neither that of a Romance nor that of an History. But it is properly hers, and you must not expect any other from her. You must imagine that she does not write but converse; and her Style and Way of Narration considered in that Light will perhaps appear at least tolerable.

However, it must be owned, that in the Course of her History, she reflects less, and relates more; but still she reflects. As she is now about to change her Station, her Recitals will consequently be more curious, and her Reflections more applicable to what passes in the Grand Monde.

As

As for the rest, many Readers perhaps will not like the Quarrel between the Coachman and Mrs Du Tour. There are People who think it beneath them to take the least Notice of what is in the common Opinion vile and ignoble. But those that are more of a Philosophic Turn, and less deceived by the Distinction which Pride has established here below; those People, I say, will be glad to see what Man is in the Character of a Coachman, and what Woman that of a petty Linnen-Draper.

THE

Lightning Source UK Ltd.
Milton Keynes UK
UKOW01f1829011217
313715UK00003B/289/P

9 781140 759515